I0813887

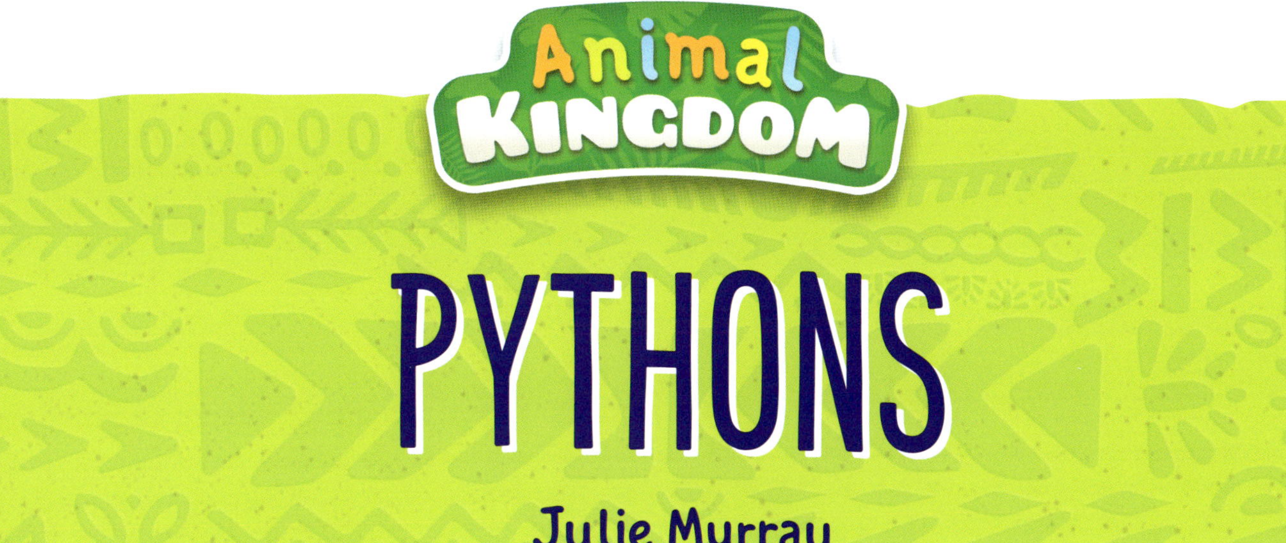

PYTHONS

Julie Murray

Big Buddy Books

An Imprint of Abdo Publishing
abdobooks.com

abdobooks.com

Published by Abdo Publishing, a division of ABDO, PO Box 398166, Minneapolis, Minnesota 55439.

Printed in the United States of America, North Mankato, Minnesota
052019
092019

Design: Sarah DeYoung, Mighty Media, Inc.
Production: Mighty Media, Inc.
Editor: Liz Salzmann
Cover Photograph: Shutterstock
Interior Photographs: Beverly Joubert/National Geographic Creative (p. 9); iStockphoto (pp. 14–15); Shutterstock (pp. 4–5, 5 (inset), 7, 10, 13, 17, 18, 19, 21 (both), 23, 24, 27, 28)

Library of Congress Control Number: 2018939892

Publisher's Cataloging-in-Publication Data
Names: Murray, Julie, author.
Title: Pythons / by Julie Murray.
Description: Minneapolis, Minnesota : Abdo Publishing, 2020. | Series: Animal kingdom | Includes online resources and index.
Identifiers: ISBN 9781532116506 (lib.bdg.) | ISBN 9781532157998 (ebook)
Subjects: LCSH: Pythons--Juvenile literature. | Constrictors (Snakes)--Juvenile literature. | Snakes--Juvenile literature. | Snakes--Behavior--Juvenile literature.
Classification: DDC 597.9678--dc23

Contents

SNAKES ARE REPTILES

Snakes, lizards, alligators, crocodiles, and turtles are all **reptiles**. Reptiles are **ectothermic** animals. Ectothermic animals cannot make heat inside their bodies.

Turtle
Python

Snakes lie in sunshine to heat themselves. They become slow when they are too cold. This is why few snakes live in cold places.

Snakes and other **reptiles** have **scaly** skin. This scaly skin keeps the reptile's body from drying out.

Are All Snakes Deadly?

Like any wild animal, snakes can be **dangerous**. Yet, most snakes are harmless. The most common snake in North America is the harmless garter snake. Harmless or not, it is best to leave wild animals alone.

PYTHONS ARE CONSTRICTORS

Pythons are **constrictor** snakes. A constrictor **squeezes** its **prey** so that it cannot breathe. This is how pythons kill their prey. Boa constrictors and anacondas are constrictors too.

A python wraps its body around its prey.

Most green tree pythons live in New Guinea.

There are about 27 kinds of pythons. They live in warm areas of **Africa**, **Australia**, **Asia**, and some Pacific islands. Pythons can live in **jungles**, **rain forests**, deserts, or **swamps**.

Most pythons live on the ground. Some pythons, like the green tree python, live mostly in trees. Other pythons live underground.

WHAT THEY LOOK LIKE

Some of the biggest snakes in the world are pythons. The reticulated python can be more than 20 feet (6 m) long. The longest snake on record was a reticulated python. It was 32 feet (10 m) long. That is as long as a school bus!

Not all pythons are big. The Children's python is only about 24 inches (61 cm) long.

The Children's python was named after British scientist John George Children.

The reticulated python lives in Asia.

Pythons can be many different colors. The reticulated python has a pattern of yellow, brown, white, gray, and black scales. The green tree python is bright green with white markings.

EATING

The python will eat almost any animal it can swallow. Snakes **stretch** their mouths wide and swallow animals whole. Some pythons can swallow a goat! But it may take a whole day for them to eat it.

A snake's jaws separate to let its mouth open wide.

Ectothermic animals such as snakes do not need to eat often. Some snakes can go months without eating.

A scrub python eating a bird

A python's meal stretches its body.

How Snakes Hear

Snakes do not hear in the same way people do. They hear by feeling **vibrations** in the ground. Snakes feel vibrations in the air too. These vibrations travel from a snake's skin to a bone in its head. A snake's **inner ear** will pick up vibrations from this bone.

When hunting, snakes sense vibrations to find prey.

GUARDING AGAINST DANGER

A python's colors and markings often match its surroundings. This **camouflage** helps pythons hide from danger.

A green tree python can hide in the leaves.

The ball python is also called the royal python.

Some pythons crawl into holes when they are **threatened**. A scared ball python will wrap itself into a tight ball. This is how the ball python got its name.

Pythons will fight back if an animal tries to hurt them. These **constrictors** can **squeeze** their enemies to death. Pythons have sharp teeth for biting too.

PYTHON BABIES

Female pythons can lay as many as 100 eggs at a time. The mother python wraps herself around her eggs to keep them safe. It takes about 100 days for the eggs to **hatch**.

Female pythons guard their eggs until they hatch.

Female pythons don't take care of the babies after they hatch.

Newly **hatched** baby pythons can leave their mothers right away. But they have to be careful and hide from other animals. Eagles and other animals will eat young pythons.

Glossary

Africa—the second-largest continent. Egypt, Libya, and Kenya are in Africa.

Asia—the largest continent. Russia, India, and China are in Asia.

Australia—the smallest continent. It includes the countries of Australia, Tasmania, and New Guinea.

camouflage (KA-muh-flahzh)—when an animal's coloring matches its surroundings. Camouflage helps animals hide.

constrictors—snakes that squeeze their prey to death.

dangerous—something that could hurt or harm.

ectothermic (ehk-tuh-THUHR-mihk)—of or related to animals that cannot make heat inside their bodies.

hatch—to be born from an egg.

inner ear—the part of the ear that is located inside the head.

jungle—an area with a lot of tropical trees and plants growing close together.

prey—an animal hunted or killed by a predator for food.

rain forest—a tropical woodland with a lot of rain.

reptile—a member of a group of living beings. Reptiles have scaly skin and are cold-blooded.

scaly—having an outer covering made up of flat plates.

squeeze—to press or grip something tightly.

stretch—to spread out to full size or greater.

swamp—land that is wet and often covered with water.

threatened—frightened by something.

vibrations—very small, quick movements back and forth.

Online Resources

To learn more about pythons, please visit **abdobooklinks.com** or scan this QR code. These links are routinely monitored and updated to provide the most current information available.

Index